Animals in My Yard

Frogs

by Amy McDonald

BELLWETHER MEDIA • MINNEAPOLIS, MN

Blastoff! Beginners are developed by literacy experts and educators to meet the needs of early readers. These engaging informational texts support young children as they begin reading about their world. Through simple language and high frequency words paired with crisp, colorful photos, Blastoff! Beginners launch young readers into the universe of independent reading.

Sight Words in This Book

a	come	little	some
and	eat	long	they
are	for	look	this
away	have	on	up
big	in	one	water
by	into	out	

This edition first published in 2022 by Bellwether Media, Inc.

No part of this publication may be reproduced in whole or in part without written permission of the publisher. For information regarding permission, write to Bellwether Media, Inc., Attention: Permissions Department, 6012 Blue Circle Drive, Minnetonka, MN 55343.

Library of Congress Cataloging-in-Publication Data

Names: McDonald, Amy, author.
Title: Frogs / by Amy McDonald.
Description: Minneapolis, MN : Bellwether Media, 2022. | Series: Animals in my yard | Includes bibliographical references and index. | Audience: Ages 4-7 | Audience: Grades K-1
Identifiers: LCCN 2021040717 (print) | LCCN 2021040718 (ebook) | ISBN 9781644875636 (library binding) | ISBN 9781648345746 (ebook)
Subjects: LCSH: Frogs--Juvenile literature.
Classification: LCC QL668.E2 M355 2022 (print) | LCC QL668.E2 (ebook) | DDC 597.8/9--dc23
LC record available at https://lccn.loc.gov/2021040717
LC ebook record available at https://lccn.loc.gov/2021040718

Text copyright © 2022 by Bellwether Media, Inc. BLASTOFF! BEGINNERS and associated logos are trademarks and/or registered trademarks of Bellwether Media, Inc.

Editor: Betsy Rathburn   Designer: Brittany McIntosh

Printed in the United States of America, North Mankato, MN.

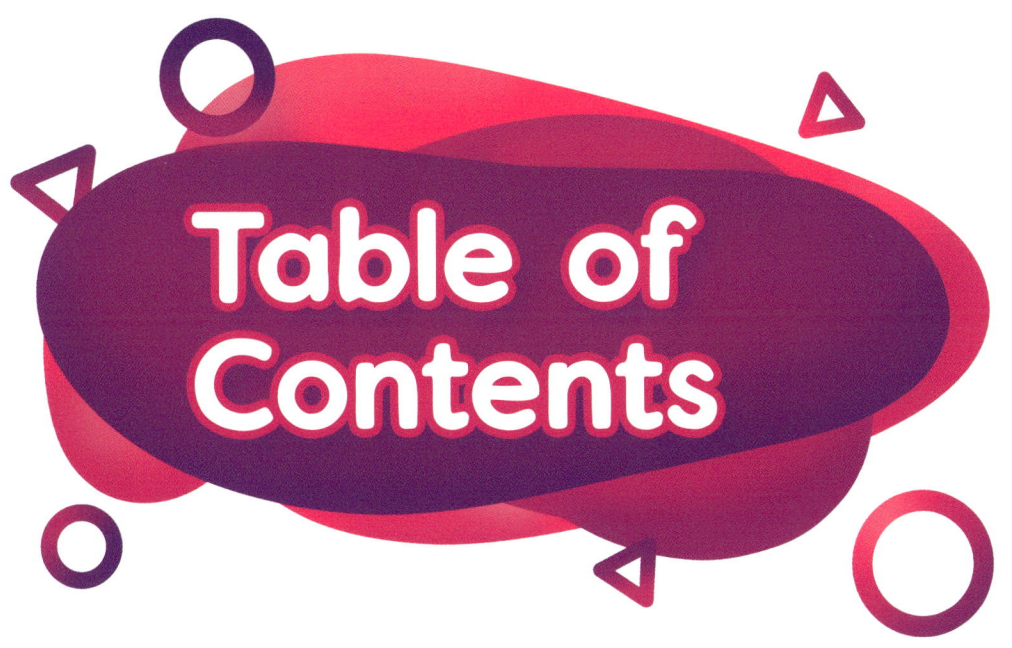

Table of Contents

Frogs!	4
Body Parts	6
The Lives of Frogs	12
Frog Facts	22
Glossary	23
To Learn More	24
Index	24

Frogs!

Ribbit, ribbit!
Hello, frog!

Body Parts

Frogs have long back legs. They hop.

leg

Frogs have big eyes. They have **smooth** skin.

skin

Frogs have sticky tongues. They snap up **prey**. Yum!

prey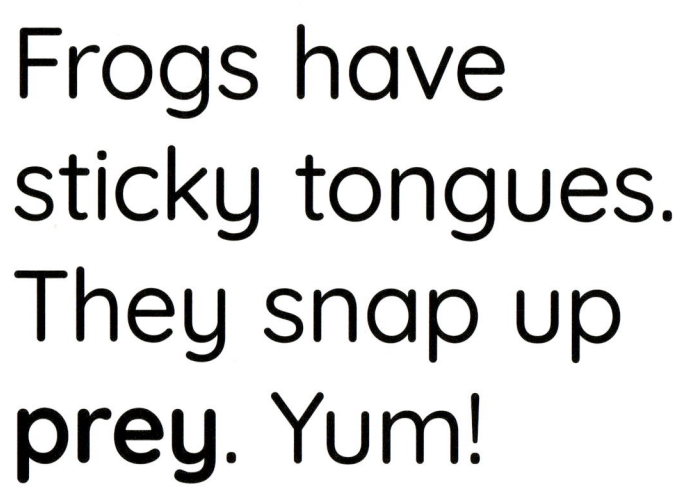

tongue

The Lives of Frogs

Frogs live by water. Some live in trees!

Frogs eat bugs and spiders. This one snacks on a worm.

bugs

spiders

worms

Frogs are food for birds and fish. Look out!

Most frogs
lay eggs in water.
Tadpoles come out!

eggs

Tadpoles grow into frogs.
Hop away, little frog!

Frog Facts

Frog Body Parts

legs • skin • eyes • tongue

Frog Food

bugs

spiders

worms

Glossary

prey

animals that are hunted

smooth

flat with no bumps

tadpoles

baby frogs

To Learn More

ON THE WEB

FACTSURFER

Factsurfer.com gives you a safe, fun way to find more information.

1. Go to www.factsurfer.com.

2. Enter "frogs" into the search box and click 🔍.

3. Select your book cover to see a list of related content.

Index

birds, 16	legs, 6, 7	worm, 14, 15
bugs, 14	prey, 10	
eat, 14	skin, 8	
eggs, 18	spiders, 14, 15	
eyes, 8, 9	tadpoles, 18, 19, 20	
fish, 16		
food, 16	tongues, 10, 11	
grow, 20	trees, 12	
hop, 6, 20	water, 12, 18	

The images in this book are reproduced through the courtesy of: IrinaK, front cover, pp. 8, 12; Michiel de Wit, pp. 3, 22; Tau5, p. 5; Mirror-Images, p. 6; spxChrome, p. 7; Angel DiBilio, p. 9; irin-k, p. 10; Christina Rollo/ Alamy, pp. 11 (tongue), 22 (tongue); Wirestock Creators, p. 13; encikAn, p. 14; waysidelynne, p. 15 (top); Andrew Balcombe, p. 15 (bottom left); Maryna Pleshkun, p. 15 (bottom right); Vladimir Turkenich, p. 17; Astrid Gast, p. 18; Savo Ilic, p. 19; Brian Magnier, p. 20; Ivan Kuzmin/ Alamy, p. 21; Margaret M Stewart, p. 22 (bugs); Claes Touber, p. 22 (spiders); Michelle Gilders/ Alamy, p. 22 (worms); LorraineHudgins, p. 23 (smooth); Joshua Ouellette, p. 23 (tadpoles).